NETWORD 2

TEACHING LANGUAGES TO ADULTS

Language games and activitie

John Langran and Sue Purcell

Cartoons by Joanne Bond

The views expressed in this publication are the authors' and do not necessarily represent those of CILT.

Acknowledgement

It is difficult to attribute authorship of different language games. Many of the games and activities in Chapter 3 have been added to and adapted by different teachers in different ways. In this list we give the name of the teacher whose work led to the game's inclusion in this book.

Sue Purcell	*Contraband, Our street, The holiday game, Who's who?, Wo bin ich?, Alibi*
John Langran	*The census, The Russian travelling salesman, I love... , Le Dourdy, The picnic*
Thorsten Friedrich	*Get in line*
Natasha Markina	*The Nobel Prize*
Celia Weber	*Le Dourdy* cartoon

The photographs were taken at a one-day CILT conference in Leicester in February 1994.

The adaptation of *The Bricklayer* story on p 53 is included by kind permission of Mrs Annetta Hoffnung.

First published 1994
© 1994 Centre for Information on Language Teaching and Research
ISBN 1 874016 23 2

Cover by Logos Design and Advertising
Printed in Great Britain by Bourne Press Ltd

Published by the Centre for Information on Language Teaching and Research, 20 Bedfordbury, Covent Garden, London WC2N 4LB.

Contents

		Page
Introduction		1
Chapter 1	WHY USE GAMES?	5
Chapter 2	HOW TO USE LANGUAGE GAMES	8
Chapter 3	A COLLECTION OF GAMES	13
Chapter 4	OLD FAVOURITES AND OTHER ACTIVITIES	44
Chapter 5	OVERCOMING RESISTANCE TO LANGUAGE GAMES	55
Chapter 6	OVER TO YOU	58
Further reading		60

List of games

Chapter 3   Games in this chapter are arranged in order, with the most basic and closely structured activity at the beginning and the most open activity at the end.

	Page
Contraband	13
Our street	15
The holiday game	17
Who's who?	19
Wo bin ich?	22
Alibi	24
The census	27
Get in line	29
The Russian travelling salesman	31
I love...	34
Le Dourdy	36
The picnic	40
The Nobel Prize	42

Chapter 4

Happy families	44
Bingo	45
Twenty questions	46
What's my line?	47
Kim's game	47
My grandmother went to market	48
Find someone who...	49
Jumbled up sentences	51
Ordering game	52

Introduction

Language games are a well-established element of foreign language teaching. Many teachers of languages to adults use language games as a standard part of their repertoire. Many of today's coursebooks suggest ways to practise and reinforce language items with various games and activities.

Language games have become particularly popular with teachers of languages to adults because:

- they give learners a real chance to speak and be creative;
- they are effective 'ice-breakers', loosening the barriers that can exist in the first lessons with a new group;
- they encourage involvement and participation;
- learners in an evening class are often tired after a hard day's work and an active approach, with language games, can be a welcome means of relaxation;
- language games encourage repetition without monotony, making practice a pleasure.

This handbook gives teachers of languages to adults a summary of reasons for using language games and a checklist of good practice and useful ideas.

This is followed by a collection of thirteen language games that the authors have found useful in the classroom. Each is an example of a principle or a strategy that can be reused or recycled with a different language or at a different level, with a different group, perhaps for a different purpose. There is also a summary of 'old favourites' and other shorter activities.

In conclusion, there are suggestions to help tutors overcome resistance to language games, an 'Over to you' section to set teachers thinking of ways to develop and adapt language games, and a list of further reading.

A language game is a device to create a situation in the classroom which gives learners the opportunity to use language they have already learnt

What is a language game?

in a relaxed way, with maximum possible free expression in order to fulfil a simple task, solve a problem or communicate a piece of information.

Games range from the very simple with strictly limited structures for beginners to fairly complicated simulations used with advanced learners for revision work.

Here is a list of some types of games and activities.

- Guessing games
  People like to make intelligent guesses, to form their own theories and to work things out by a process of elimination. This can be used as a motivating factor in a language game.

- Memory games
  People like testing their memory. This gives you a challenge and can make you think in the language you are learning. See if you can remember as much about a picture as other people in the group.

- Putting things in order
  Many things have a natural order or sequence, but to remember a logical sequence can be an exciting challenge.

- Comparing pictures - finding differences
  An effective way of generating conversation in pairs. Find a suitable picture and photocopy it with alterations. Then ask learners to find the differences by talking to each other without looking at each other's pictures.

- Comparing notes with other learners
  Like picture differences, but with text. In pairs, each partner has the same set of notes but one has been changed. Find the differences by asking each other questions.

- Information gap games
  Many language games contain 'information gaps'. The object is to find the information you need from another member of the group.

- Filling in a diary/calendar
  Planning your time can be a challenge, especially when you have to make arrangements that fit in with those of others in the group. This can be used effectively as a basis for games involving the language of arranging meetings and planning trips.

- Collaborating to complete a task
  Many activities can be given to small groups as a joint task. This encourages individuals to make a contribution, and the need to get the task completed adds a sense of urgency to the work.

- Word games
  Games can be used to manipulate words and text, for example in word bingo.

- Simulations
  When fully developed, the language game can become a full simulation, with the classroom transformed into an imaginary scenario and learners taking their own independent roles.

- Ice-breakers
  A large number of games can be used to break down barriers that may exist, for example, the tenseness at the start of a lesson or a short course. Language games get learners talking to each other.

As you will see in Chapter 3, many games involve more than one of these 'ingredients'.

The games in this book are intended to be adapted for use with any language that you may be teaching, and examples are given mainly in English, French, German and Russian. Different languages will present their own difficulties in particular language areas, and therefore we have

How to use this book

not necessarily specified the level at which a particular game should be used. Additionally, many language games can be reused at different levels; the level of difficulty will depend on the framework set by the teacher.

We have tried to choose games which are transferable and can be used for any language. If the language you teach does not figure in our examples, we hope you will still consider using the techniques we are recommending, adapting the ideas for your particular situation.

Will these games work for you?

The games have been included because they have worked well for the authors at different times with different groups. This does not necessarily mean that they will all work for you with your groups in exactly the way that we have presented them here. Different teachers work in different ways; some are good at running an activity from the front of the class, others are good at managing groups. Some are good at both. Hopefully there is sufficient material here to give you ideas about how to develop your own particular strengths and work on any weaknesses.

Why use games?

Chapter 1

- Games simulate a real-life situation.
- Language used in games is used for a purpose; it is relevant and meaningful.
- Games can be used at all levels and to practise almost any structure or area of vocabulary.
- Games are a useful strategy for revision.
- Games help learners to ask questions.
- When you use language games, learners speak more and this leads to confidence. The shyer learners are less threatened than if they have to speak in front of the whole class.
- Games are good fun and can help you create a relaxed, friendly and co-operative atmosphere in your groups.
- Games are an effective way of learning.
- Games can be useful examination practice.

*Games simulate a
real-life situation*

Most adults who learn a language do so in order to be able to use it, usually more or less immediately, to travel abroad or to meet foreign visitors at home. They therefore want to be able to function in real situations, to find ways of saying what they need to say and to make themselves understood when they don't necessarily 'know all the words'. Language games can give them these opportunities and virtually any situation that people are likely to find themselves in can be effectively simulated.

If most adults learn a language in order to use it, they will see the value of intensive practice in a simulated real-life situation. Being able to use the language early on in the course to achieve a realistic task is a very effective spur to motivation. Learners are able to rehearse in the classroom the situations they will meet when they travel.

*Games involve
relevant and
meaningful language*

Games can be used to practise all four skills - listening, speaking, reading and writing - and to integrate them. Most language classes for adults in the UK emphasise practical oral skills. Therefore this book concentrates on communicative games to aid conversational skills, with the focus on

Games are versatile

listening and speaking. All types of communicative activity can be developed, e.g. asking and answering questions, agreeing and disagreeing, approving and disapproving, explaining and describing, counting and checking, buying and selling. Language games can be used at all levels, and to practise any structure or area of vocabulary.

Games aid revision

Many adult classes meet just once a week and for these groups it is useful to have ways of reusing language learnt the previous week; language games provide a way of doing this. They can be used to practise language covered in previous lessons, even previous years, in a different context.

Many courses are cyclic in structure, with the same situations being reworked at different stages of the course. A language game is an effective way of reviving language learnt in the past.

Games help learners ask questions

When you travel abroad, a lot of your language activity is asking questions to find out things you need to know. Many travellers find they are not very good at this because in the traditional classroom it is usually the teacher who asks the questions and the learners who give the answers. Language games can reverse this. With a problem to solve in the classroom, the learners get plenty of practice at asking questions, either of each other or of the teacher.

Games let learners speak more

If the teacher works from the front of the class, asking questions, he or she speaks perhaps for half the time. The individual learners have their own fraction of the time that is left. In a large group this can be just a few minutes. One of the most common criticisms of an adult language course is *I didn't get a chance to speak*.

Language games, played in pairs or small groups, can give learners the chance to speak for a far larger proportion of the time available, and the more nervous students feel less inhibited when they are not being listened to by the whole group. Learners also listen to each other more to complete the task in hand. The teacher generally takes a background role and learners gain in confidence as they realise that they can cope in a real situation by themselves.

Language games are an effective approach for 'conversation classes', where learners come to a weekly meeting with the intention of maintaining their level of language and developing their speaking skills.

Teachers of such groups need to find a variety of scenarios for language use, rather than just asking learners to talk about a particular theme.

Games provide variety, raise motivation, and maintain interest. At the beginning of a course, language games will help you create a friendly, participative atmosphere right from the start. Language games will ensure that people don't always sit in the same seat, perhaps never even speaking to some other members of the group. Particularly in the evening, after a hard day at work, probably spent sitting down, adult learners look forward to coming to a class in which they will spend at least a proportion of their time standing up, moving around and actively participating in a group activity. When you stand up to do something in a classroom you actually **feel** different. The lessons are more enjoyable for everyone, learners will look forward to coming to classes and will be less likely to drop out. Learners who have enjoyed learning together are likely to have better social relationships and to give each other greater support, when this is needed.

Games are fun

We know that learning is most effective when made enjoyable and functional, and we know that language learning is more likely to work when there is a large amount of meaningful repetition. Both these conditions can be achieved in a language programme using carefully chosen and well thought-out games as the main technique for practising the language that is being learnt.

Games are an effective way of learning

Up-to-date examination syllabuses include a large proportion of role play situations for which learners can be effectively prepared with a programme of structured language games. Fluency, confidence, and the ability to improvise are useful in the examination role play.

Games provide examination preparation

How to use language games

Chapter 2

Most teachers use language games as standard practice. Often they have one or two favourites which they use at different stages of the course and for different purposes. The greatest problem is deciding which game is right for your group in any particular lesson, and then planning it carefully, judging the logistics and allocating the right amount of time.

Here is a checklist of points to bear in mind when planning and using language games.

- ❑ Define the structures and vocabulary
- ❑ Choose a relevant topic
- ❑ Check the logistics
- ❑ Make sure the room is suitable
- ❑ Prepare the activity
- ❑ Look for opportunities for 'pyramid' work
- ❑ Check for key words
- ❑ Make sure the instructions are clear
- ❑ Demonstrate, if necessary
- ❑ Set the scene
- ❑ Maximise ownership and choice
- ❑ During the activity - monitor, prompt, be on hand
- ❑ Stop the game at the right time
- ❑ Look for effective follow-up
- ❑ Make sure learners understand why you have decided to use language games as a teaching strategy
- ❑ Introduce games early on in a beginners' class

Define structures and vocabulary

Often you will want a language game to reinforce a particular language structure or area of vocabulary which has recently been introduced. In this case you need to make sure that what you are asking learners to do actually requires them to use this language and not other language, which they have not yet met. Make sure that you have practised the forms which are needed, that learners know how to pronounce everything reasonably well, and that they can produce any written forms that are needed, for example in workcards which they have to fill in during the game.

It is important that the situations and topics which you choose should be relevant to your learners and their future use of the language, at least most of the time. Language games are most effective when the relevance is direct and immediate and this is of course particularly important for language courses for business when the language used can be related to the learner's job. Many language games rely on learners comparing information about themselves: knowledge, facts or opinions, and this can greatly enhance motivation.

Choose a relevant topic

Many language games rely on interacting pairs and groups. It is very important to check that what you are asking people to do will actually work smoothly. For example, in THE RUSSIAN TRAVELLING SALESMAN activity (page 31) the number of towns that you use will depend on the number of people in your group. If you use too many in this case, learners will find it difficult to find partners and the result will be frustration. Be careful that the tasks you set are actually achievable within a simple and understandable framework. Check the timing carefully. It is easy to underestimate how long a language game will actually take.

Check the logistics

Learners often need to take notes while they are moving around talking to different people. It is useful to have a set of small clipboards available for this purpose, or use worksheets on card instead of paper. Thin card will go through most photocopiers and printers.

Ideally, a language classroom for a teacher who uses a lot of language games should have a formal area for learners to sit, with or without tables, and a flexible area where they can stand or sit, and move around, depending on the activity. The strategy suggested for exploiting picture differences (page 36), for example, requires first several groups of four to eight learners, then random pairs, then groups again, then the whole class working together. It is asking a lot for every adult language classroom to be this flexible, and many are not. If you plan to use an active approach that requires learners to move around the room, you should make this known before rooms are allocated. If the room you are given is not suitable, can you rearrange it? Or can you have the active part of the work take place somewhere else? If you have a particularly ambitious activity for a particular lesson, perhaps you can book the hall.

Use a suitable room

Room 302 at Brasshouse Centre, Birmingham, an ideal room for language games. The chairs are in a horseshoe, and there is plenty of room to stand and move about. There is a pinboard on the wall for workcards, and the whiteboard and the cassette recorder trolley are on wheels for flexibility.

Prepare the activity

Some language games, particularly those that use role-cards, require detailed preparation which can take a lot of time. For example, to prepare THE CENSUS (page 27) you have to have a role-card ready for each member of the group. Other activities, such as THE PICNIC (page 40), are less demanding on preparation of this sort, but the teacher still needs a careful note of the sequencing of the activity, the instructions to give and the vocabulary to use.

Look for opportunities for 'pyramid' work

This is the term used for a technique that forces people to commit themselves to a point of view or find out information, and then use this in further discussions in a bigger group. For example, decide in pairs where you want to go for lunch. Then combine three pairs into groups of six and try to agree again. First, people commit themselves to something, then they have to make out a case for it and convince others about it. In this book groups are manipulated in this way in several activities, especially LE DOURDY (page 36) and THE PICNIC.

Check for key words

In most language games there will be a few key words that are essential to success. Learners need to be able to catch people's attention, introduce themselves and say things like *Excuse me, please*; *Sorry, could you say that again*; *No, I'm not the person you are looking for*. As your group uses more language games, learners will build up a stock of such phrases. In the early stages they will have to be practised specially.

It is essential that learners should understand what they are expected to do, and how they are expected to do it. When manipulating groups, you can cause uncertainty and chaos with inadequate or unclear instructions. To play the game, people need to know the rules. Explain these as clearly as possible. Which language to use for your explanation will depend on the group. If the instructions are simple and the group will be able to cope with them, you will want to use the foreign language. If they are complicated, you may decide to use English to save time. Or you may decide to give instructions in the foreign language and then again in English as a check.

Give clear instructions - demonstrate if necessary

Often you will need to demonstrate some of the situations in front of the whole class with one or two learners, before you can start the game. Another useful strategy is to allow the game to start before everyone has fully understood what is needed, and then stop everything after about 30 seconds. Then allow, for example, one pair to continue, check in front of the whole group that they are actually doing what is needed, and ask everyone to continue. At all times you need to maintain firm control; never be afraid to stop the activity to explain a point which people are getting badly wrong.

In the more involved activities or simulations, it helps to take care setting the scene, where possible using dramatic techniques to maximise the affective appeal of the situation. In THE RUSSIAN TRAVELLING SALESMAN (page 31) you do this by describing in detail just how difficult the life of a Russian salesman can be.

Set the scene

You will increase motivation if you give your learners the opportunity to make their own choices, whenever possible. For example, in THE PICNIC (page 40) learners can decide themselves what they are taking on the picnic. This is then something they **want** to take, and talking about it is more important to them. They **own** it. However, when working with near-beginner groups you usually have to limit the vocabulary more carefully. One way of doing this is to ask learners to choose a role-card, which tells them the part they have to play in the activity.

Maximise ownership and choice

Be on hand during the activity

While the game is actually taking place the teacher can to some extent relax! The point is that in normal oral language teaching, when you are at the front of the class, you are constantly the focus of the action, interacting with individual students or the whole group. Whereas when the class is involved in a language game, you move out of the centre of the stage. You can decide either to move around, listening and prompting, taking notes of particular points that need emphasising or correcting later on, or to concentrate on the work of a particular learner. You should monitor the work sensitively, without inhibiting it. Don't stop the flow by constant correction.

You can also take time out to prepare something for the next stage of the lesson.

Decide when to stop the game

Some language games come to a natural end in a group activity. With others it is more difficult. In pair work, some pairs will finish before others. You do not want people sitting around waiting for others to finish. It is useful to have some extra activities ready for this moment, perhaps to ask any learners who finish early to rehearse a dialogue from the game to perform in front of the class. A general rule is to stop the game too soon rather than too late.

Plan some form of follow-up

Most language games lend themselves to some form of follow-up. A pair work activity leads naturally to verbal interaction, with different pairs giving their results. A summary of the results of a language game can be used as a reading or listening exercise. Most games lead to effective written work if this is one of your aims.

Explain your strategy

Adult learners need to know how they learn and it will help if at some stage you explain the thinking behind the strategies you adopt, and the purpose of particular activities as you use them. It is probably not a good idea, though, to discuss new methods with a group before they have had some experience of working with them.

Use games early on in a beginners' class

Language games, if well structured with carefully limited vocabulary, can be used from the very first lessons of a beginners' course. In general, the earlier such techniques are used the better, before learning patterns become fixed.

A collection of games

Chapter 3

Type: Guessing game	**CONTRABAND**
Timing: 5-10 minutes	*by Sue Purcell*

★ To practise asking and answering yes/no questions.   PURPOSE

★ Present tense of verb 'to have' in various languages. Useful for   LANGUAGE ELEMENTS
practising *some* and *any* in English, *du, de la, de l', des* and *de* in
positive and negative sentences in French, *del, della, dell', degli* and
dei in Italian, and *kein* in German.

Draw up a list of ten or twelve items for each student (see example   **PREPARATION**
below).

For the French version the tutor will introduce *du, de la*, etc by showing   **PRE-TEACHING**
pictures or realia which include masculine, feminine and plural nouns
and perhaps asking *Qu'est-ce que vous avez à déclarer?* To practise the use
of *de* after a negative, show, for example, a picture of a bottle of wine
and ask *Est-ce que vous avez de la bière?*.

- Tell the students that they are trying to   **ACTIVITY**
  smuggle three items through customs.
- Give each student a list of ten or twelve
  items.
- Ask them to choose which three they are
  smuggling.
- In pairs, students have to try to find out
  which items their partner has ticked by
  asking *Avez-vous des cigarettes?* and so on.
  The reply is either *Non, je n'ai pas de
  cigarettes* or *Oui, j'ai des cigarettes*.

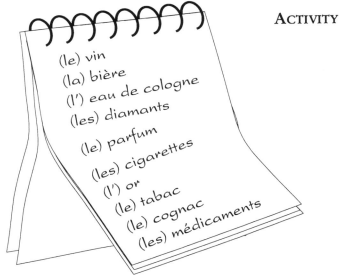

(le) vin
(la) bière
(l') eau de cologne
(les) diamants
(le) parfum
(les) cigarettes
(l') or
(le) tabac
(le) cognac
(les) médicaments

FOLLOW-UP

The teacher could, for example, get the group to give an oral summary of who smuggled what, or the class could produce this for a written homework.

VARIATIONS

This activity can be adapted to cover any area of vocabulary merely by changing the context, e.g. guess:

★ *Three things I've got in my handbag.*
★ *Three things I've got in my living room.*
★ *Three things I've got in my fridge.*

It is particularly useful with more advanced classes when working with specialised areas of vocabulary. It can also be adapted to different tenses, e.g. guess three things your partner used to do when he was young, would do if he was rich, etc.

The CONTRABAND scenario can be adapted to a whole-class activity by giving each student a picture of just one item which he or she is trying to smuggle. Each student is also playing the role of customs official and has three guesses to find out what item each 'traveller' is smuggling. Students must hand over their picture if the 'customs officer' guesses correctly. The winner is the student who has collected the most cards by the end of the game or by a certain time.

Type: Information gap **Timing:** Approx 10 minutes	OUR STREET *by Sue Purcell*

★ To find out, using very simple language, the number of the house everyone lives in, to practise simple present tense questions and answers combined with numbers.

PURPOSE

★ This activity can be played very early on in a beginners' course as it only involves asking someone's name and the number of their house. Useful in French for practising the tricky numbers 70-99 and in Spanish for practising numbers where the pronunciation is close and easily confused, e.g. 60-*sesenta*, 70-*setenta*.

LANGUAGE ELEMENTS

For each student, prepare a copy of the Chestnut Avenue street plan and an individual role-card showing names, faces and house numbers. If there are more than twelve students in the class, make extra role-cards; two or more characters can live in the same house. If there are fewer, some of the houses can be empty.

PREPARATION

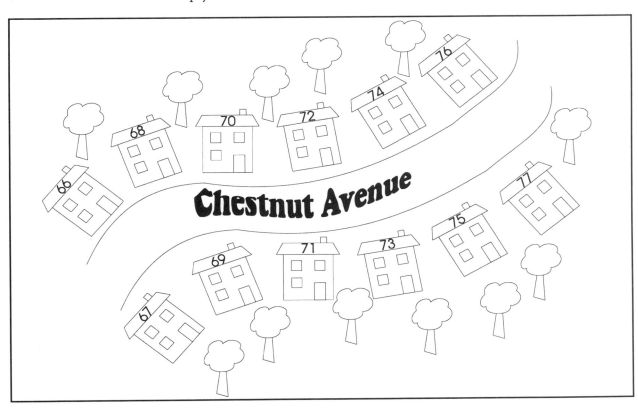

No. 72	No. 75	No. 70	No. 67	No. 69	No. 74
Mcheshi Kioko	Premila Patel	Stephen Burns	Helen Davies	Ray Edwards	John Kinnear
No. 71	No. 66	No. 76	No. 73	No. 77	No. 68
Harry Gardiner	Mazhar Ahmed	Melanie Smith	Susan Chan	Colin Read	Margaret Day

PRE-TEACHING The game can be played when the numbers used for Chestnut Avenue have just been introduced. As the class progresses to higher, more difficult numbers, the figures in the street plan can be changed. Make sure the class knows the simple questions *What is your name?* and *Where do you live?*

ACTIVITY The students move around the class trying to fit a name to each house in Chestnut Avenue.

FOLLOW-UP When the exercise has been completed and the students have their own lists of who lives where, you can read out a version with one or two mistakes for them to spot and correct. Learners with more vocabulary can question each other about who their neighbours are, who lives opposite, etc. Or ask for a written summary, if desired.

VARIATIONS Other information can be added to the role-cards, e.g. age, profession, thus increasing the number of questions the students can ask.

Consider also not distributing any information at all about one of the houses. Ask the question *What number of house does Fred Smith live in?* When they have asked everyone in the class the learners will be left with just one house for which they have no information. By a process of elimination they will have found out where Fred Smith lives.

Also, of course, there is no need to use fictitious names, especially if you are working with a group who are very shortly going to travel abroad and will have to talk about themselves a lot. If you do ask people to use their own names, make sure they know how to pronounce these in the foreign language.

Type: Matching roles	THE HOLIDAY GAME
Timing: Approx 15 minutes	*by Sue Purcell*

★ To find a person with similar interests and preferences to yourself and with whom you could happily go on holiday. — PURPOSE

★ Useful for practising conditional tense of verbs expressing desire and preference, such as *je voudrais/aimerais/préférerais* in French, *vorrei, amerei, preferirei* in Italian and *I'd like* in English. Also useful in German for practising the position of the infinitive after *ich möchte*. Present or future tenses can be used instead, if preferred. The follow-up activity incorporates the language of making suggestions. — LANGUAGE ELEMENTS

No student material needed. Make a handy checklist of different types of holidays for yourself. — **PREPARATION**

Make sure that learners are familiar with both the first and second person forms of the tenses of the verbs you intend to use and can ask open questions in the relevant tense, *Qu'est-ce que vous voudriez faire....?* etc. As students come up with suggestions (see below) you can practise the phrases in an appropriate sentence. — **PRE-TEACHING**

Elicit from the class three places to stay on holiday, three ways of travelling and three things they like doing on holiday. Make sure that the choices are sufficiently dissimilar to represent a range of tastes and preferences, e.g: — **ACTIVITY**

★ Camping; hotel; a local family.
★ Train and boat; plane; own car.
★ Go round museums and art galleries; lie on beach; go for country walks.

Ask learners to imagine their preferred holiday by making one choice from each section. They must then question their classmates - e.g. in Spanish *¿Dónde te gustaría quedarte?*, *¿Qué te gustaría hacer durante tus vacaciones?*, *Where would you like to stay? What would you like to do on holiday?* - to see if they can find anyone with similar preferences to be their holiday companion. If learners cannot find an ideal match they may negotiate and compromise.

When learners find a possible companion or companions they can get together and plan their 'holiday' in more detail:

★ *Shall we go to Seville?*	*¿Vamos a Sevilla?*
★ *We could go to Salamanca.*	*Podríamos ir a Salamanca.*
★ *When shall we go?*	*¿Cuándo iremos?*
★ *How long shall we stay?*	*¿Cuánto tiempo estaremos allí?*

VARIATIONS

Extra categories could be added or could replace those above, particularly if you wish to practise a special vocabulary area or structure, e.g. time of year you wish to travel, how you intend to spend your evenings, preferred climate, etc.

Any context where learners have to find a partner with similar tastes or characteristics can be adopted for this format. Learners supply a range of suggestions before making their own three or four choices from the list. Finding a flatmate, sharing an office or a 'lonely hearts' theme all lead to discussion on habits such as smoking and tidiness as well as on hobbies and interests.

You can of course make the exercise a freer one by not limiting the choices and asking students to be themselves. An interesting variation is to put students into groups of four. Tell them that they had agreed to go on holiday together (or share a flat), but then find that there are only three places left on the trip (or only room for three in the flat). They then have to agree on who is going to leave the group and why.

Type: Information gap Timing: 10-15 minutes	WHO'S WHO? *by Sue Purcell*
★ To question your partner about the identity and job title of people for whom you only have a physical description. An appropriate activity for general business language training.	PURPOSE
	LANGUAGE ELEMENTS
★ In the example given, questions are put in the simple present tense to practise adjectives, personal descriptions and job titles.	

Prepare enough role-cards for your group - plus a few extras in case you need them.

PREPARATION

Introduce or revise the vocabulary either by asking learners to describe each other or by talking about pictures and flashcards. The advantage of pictures is that no one is embarrassed at being labelled 'fat' or 'old' by their classmates.

PRE-TEACHING

Make sure that learners know how to ask and answer questions in the third person, e.g.:

★ *Wie heißt der Mann mit der Brille?*
★ *Comment s'appelle la femme avec les cheveux longs?*
★ *Chi è la donna bassa con gli occhiali?*
★ *¿Cómo se llama el hombre alto?*
★ *She is called...*

Divide the class into pairs. Set the scene. Partner A has just arrived to work in a new firm. He/she has seen various people, but doesn't know their names or their jobs. Partner B, who knows everyone, listens to partner A's description and puts names and job titles to them.

ACTIVITY

It is important that the pictures on the two cards are arranged in a different order, otherwise learners may just read from left to right. Make sure they don't look at each other's cards.

Partner A

You have just arrived at your company's small British headquarters where you will be working on secondment for the next few weeks. While sitting in reception you see the people pictured below pass through and realise that they will be your colleagues. Eventually you are collected and welcomed by your British counterpart and you question him/her as to the identity of the people you have just seen. Describe the people below and fill in their name and position within the company.

Name _____ _____ _____ _____ _____ _____

Position _____ _____ _____ _____ _____ _____

Partner B

You have been asked to look after an employee from your overseas branch who will be working with you for the next few weeks. When you pick him/her up from reception, listen to the description of the people he/she saw while waiting. From the descriptions say who those people were.

Simon Edwards
Chief
Accountant

Tim Roberts
Deputy
Finance Director

Carol Frost
Chairman's
Secretary

Ted Halliday
Production Manager

Ian Brown
Vice Chairman

Helen Green
Marketing Director

For listening work based on the same pictures, the teacher can read the descriptions and make mistakes which the class points out. Written follow-up can be devised if necessary. For example:

Here is a note that a visitor to the firm made about people he met, but he had a very full day and didn't recall everything perfectly. Make any necessary corrections:

Simon Edwards, the Vice Chairman, is short with a black beard... etc.

For this exercise it may be most effective to take away the pictures and ask learners to work from memory.

If you have young children you may have met a board game called *Guess who?* by MB Games. This uses the theme of personal descriptions very effectively and is extremely useful for language practice when all the vocabulary for describing faces has been introduced. There are two boards each with 30 faces on flaps. Each player has one person whose identity he has to find. Players ask alternate questions to eliminate people from the search.

To avoid just one of the pair asking all the questions, the information can be split between the two role-cards and both partners can take turns in asking for and supplying information. Perhaps they have both been at the firm a week and each knows some colleagues but not others.

You can add more detailed information to the pictures, for example how long people have been working with the company, what their strengths and weaknesses are, who they get on with, etc.

WO BIN ICH? *by Sue Purcell*	Type: Guessing game Timing: 5-10 minutes

PURPOSE	★ To practise asking and answering yes/no questions.
LANGUAGE ELEMENTS	★ Post-beginners level. Useful in German to practise modal verbs and their effect on word order. Useful in French for practising the position of the pronoun *y* by asking *Est-ce qu'on peut y acheter du pain?* etc.

PREPARATION

Prepare a set of picture cards for each group, showing a variety of places, e.g. library, post-office, café, theatre, etc (see samples below). This game is a version of TWENTY QUESTIONS (see page 46), which requires less preparation. Using cards here enables you to control the vocabulary, adds interest and speeds up the tempo of play within the small groups.

Swimming pool

Restaurant

Supermarket

Library

Theatre

Prison

Zoo

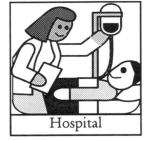
Hospital

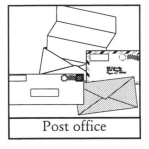
Post office

PRE-TEACHING

For the German version this game is intended to be used after the introduction of the present tense of the modal verbs *können*, *müssen* and *dürfen*. Learners will need to know that these verbs send the infinitive to the end of the sentence.

You can begin by asking questions about the towns where the students live:

★ *Kann man dort Tennis spielen?*
★ *Kann man gut einkaufen?*
★ *Was kann man abends dort machen?*

Then you can show a picture of one of the places to be used later and elicit the appropriate questions.

This game is best played in groups of three or four so that everyone has a turn to ask and answer questions. It is also a useful pair work activity.

One learner picks a card without showing it to the others in the group. They have to guess which place it is by asking yes/no questions using modal verbs, e.g.:

★ *Kann man dort Brot kaufen?*
★ *Darf man dort rauchen?*
★ *Muß man bezahlen, dorthin zu gehen?*
★ *Also, sind Sie im Theater?*

The main teaching point is the structure being used in the question, probably modal verbs. However, students are likely to need to ask questions using words they don't know. Encourage them to ask you for help or use a dictionary, or both.

Use pictures of different countries cut from travel agents' brochures to extend vocabulary.

★ *Kann man dort skilaufen?*
★ *Darf man dort Alkohol trinken?*

Instead of modal verbs, the same pictures can be used to practise the past tense. Students try and guess where the others have just been on holiday.

★ *Haben Sie dort Chianti getrunken?*
★ *Haben Sie ein Kängeruh dort gesehen?*

ALIBI _by Sue Purcell_	**Type:** Information gap **Timing:** 15-20 minutes
PURPOSE	★ To practise asking and answering questions in the past tenses, particularly the imperfect tense. Learners have to check each other's alibi for a particular time, and find any inconsistencies.
LANGUAGE ELEMENTS	★ Any language. For intermediate groups who have had a thorough introduction to the imperfect tense, or are revising it, and who have enough vocabulary to be able to cope with the necessary detail. For more elementary classes you can prepare alibis which only involve the use of the verb 'to be', particularly in Spanish to drill the use of the imperfect tense of _estar_.

PRE-TEACHING

The imperfect tense. In French, for example, the _je_, _nous_ and _vous_ forms will need drilling or thorough revision. Make sure the students can ask the question _Qu'est-ce que vous faisiez samedi dernier à 8 heures?_

ACTIVITY

A game for the whole class. Explain that a crime has been committed and the whole class are suspects. The members have to check each other's alibis, looking for inconsistencies to try to find the criminal.

There is a set of role-cards for a French class of twelve people opposite. Clearly you will often need some last-minute adjustment, depending on how many people come to the lesson. For example, if eleven people arrive on this occasion, remove Hélène's card and change Pierre's alibi to _un aperitif au bar 'Europa' avec collègues Sylvie et Henri_, and add Pierre's name to Henri and Sylvie's alibi. Or, to make things easier, you can have a few spare cards ready for people who were on their own.

Each learner is given a card with the basic information concerning his or her whereabouts, for example at 8 o'clock last Saturday evening. Learners must ask everyone else in the class what they were doing at that time, make notes, then finally check to see whose alibi is inconsistent and who is therefore the prime suspect.

HENRI
un aperitif au bar 'Europa' avec collègue Sylvie

MARIE
cinéma, film 'Cyrano de Bergerac' avec amie Chantal

PIERRE
dîner au restaurant 'Saint Gourmand' avec amie Hélène

MONIQUE
film à la télévision, à la maison, seule

SYLVIE
un aperitif au bar 'Europa' avec collègue Henri

HÉLÈNE
dîner au restaurant 'Saint Gourmand' avec ami Pierre

CHANTAL
cinéma, film 'Cyrano de Bergerac' avec amie Marie

CHARLES
dîner à la maison avec Ghislaine

CLAUDE
tennis au club avec Robert

MICHELLE
dîner au restaurant 'Saint Gourmand' avec Monique

GHISLAINE
dîner chez Charles

ROBERT
tennis au club avec Claude

The activity is more realistic if learners use name labels, perhaps handwritten sticky labels. You can then ask them not to approach their own alibi. Otherwise, their first question to everyone should be *Comment vous appelez-vous?*

In addition to an individual role-card explaining their alibi, each learner gets a copy of the grid below which he or she must fill in with the information obtained from classmates.

Qui?	Où?	Avec qui?	Vrai/faux?
Henri			
Marie			
Pierre			
Monique			
Sylvie			
Hélène			
Chantal			
Charles			
Claude			
Michelle			
Ghislaine			
Robert			

FOLLOW-UP

To round off the activity, you can ask the class general questions using different tenses, such as:

★ *A votre avis, qui a tué la personne?*
★ *Qui mentait?*
★ *Qui est le coupable?/le meurtrier?*
★ *Comment savez-vous cela?*

And you can ask learners to write up a report of their investigation for homework.

VARIATIONS

CLAUDE
7h   arrivée au club
7 - 9h tennis
9h   bière au bar
10h   départ du club

The amount of information on the role-cards can be increased to encourage the use of more verbs and other tenses. You can make the period as long as you like, from ten minutes to a whole week. Usually a smaller group should have more items to check and a larger group should have fewer.

For a more advanced group you can use the format of the traditional party game ALIBI. Two members of the class prepare a detailed, matching alibi out of earshot of the rest of the class. Tell the remainder of the group that they are the detectives. Have them prepare their questions and then interview the two suspects in turn, looking for inconsistencies in their accounts.

Type: Information gap	**THE CENSUS**
Timing: Approx 10 minutes	*by John Langran*

★ Intensive practice of questions and answers concerning personal identity.   PURPOSE

★ Simple questions and answers incorporating different intonation patterns.   LANGUAGE ELEMENTS

PREPARATION

Prepare a set of simple identity role-cards for half of the group (samples below). For the other half, prepare a summary of the information in the third person, but with a number of simple mistakes, at least one for each card. Any word processor will speed up this preparation considerably.

Identity cards for the census, which need translating into the language you are teaching:

You are:	You are:	You are:
Ivan Ivanov	Natasha Kurchenko	Vladimir Minsky
Scientist	Company Director	Mechanic
Married	Single	Married
One daughter	38 years old	Two sons
47 years old		27 years old

Census data to be checked:

Ivan Ivanov	Natasha Kurchenko	Vladimir Minsky
Scientist	Company Secretary	Mechanic
Married	Single	Married
Two daughters	34 years old	Two daughters
47 years old		27 years old

PRE-TEACHING

Practise questions relating to all the material on the cards. Pay particular attention to the intonation patterns that are used in a follow-up question when the first answer you have had is not what you requested.

For example:	*You are Ivan Ivanov?*	*Yes.*
	You are a scientist?	*Yes.*
	You are married?	*Yes.*
	You have two daughters?	*No, I have one daughter.*
	Just one daughter?	*Yes, one daughter.*

ACTIVITY

Divide the class into two groups. Give one group the identity cards and ask them to prepare to talk about their new identity. Give the other group the census results.

Set the scene. There has been a census, but a lot of the results have been wrongly recorded, perhaps because a computer operator was not sober at the workplace. The task is for the census workers to check the results which they have been given, and correct them where necessary.

Ask learners to move around and talk to each other. The census workers ask the questions, using both direct interrogatives and yes/no type questions as appropriate. Clearly the activity is more demanding for the census workers than for those holding the cards. It may be a good idea to play the game twice, swapping roles. There is no need to wait until everyone has finished. When people have completed about 60% of their work you can bring the whole group together for a round-up of the results to fill in everyone's gaps.

VARIATIONS

Both this activity and ALIBI demonstrate how an information gap situation can be created very simply and effectively, using role-cards with slight differences.

The same technique can be reapplied in different scenarios, imaginary and real. One interesting pair work activity is to compare menus from the same restaurant, one up to date, one a few years old. How have prices changed? How has the menu changed? Has it improved or deteriorated?

Type: Ordering game	GET IN LINE
Timing: 5-10 minutes	*by Thorsten Friedrich**

★ An activity that gets learners moving around, particularly useful as a warm-up activity at the start of a short course, such as a weekend course, where you want people to get to know each other quickly, or at any stage where you want intensive practice of a new structure which can be used with comparisons or some sort of measurement. Our example 'How well do you understand computers?' would be useful for a group of business people at the start of a short revision course.

PURPOSE

★ Simple questions and answers, plus intensive practice of comparisons. For example, when two learners are deciding whether or not they should be ahead of each other in the row, they need to decide who knows more about computers, with sentences such as *I understand Windows better than you do* or *I use electronic mail more often than you do.*

LANGUAGE ELEMENTS

Prepare a reference list of the vocabulary that the learners will need to discuss the topic you have chosen. You can give this to the learners as a hand-out, but it will often be more effective to elicit the words from the group at the beginning of the session, writing them on the board as you go.

PREPARATION

Thorough pre-teaching of a new structure. Reminders of essential points when revising.

PRE-TEACHING

For our example 'How well do you understand computers?', learners need to be able to ask the questions and give answers such as *quite well*, *not very well at all* and so on, and use certain comparisons. As well as this, for our example, those who do know something about computers will have to be able to ask and answer questions such as:

★ *Have you got a computer/printer at home?*
★ *Have you got a notebook/laptop etc?*
★ *Do you use a word processor/database?*
★ *Do you use Windows?*

---

*   Thorsten Friedrich is a lecturer in English at the Volkshochschule Frankfurt.

ACTIVITY

Ask the learners to stand in one, two, three or four lines, according to the size of the group. Then ask them to get in order within their lines, with the person who understands computers best at the front and the person who understands them least at the back. They do this by talking to people in front and behind them and agreeing to change places if necessary.

LOGISTICS

You must have sufficient space for the whole group to stand in two or more lines and move around. The lines don't need to be very long - perhaps five or six people. Some people may guess where they should be in the line and go straight there. This may speed things up.

One way of getting people to stand in random lines to start this game is to give them numbers, or days of the week, or months of the year, or anything with a fixed order. For example, to make three equal lines, tell the first three learners that they are Monday, the next three Tuesday, then Wednesday, etc. Ask all the Mondays to come to the front of the class. Then ask the others to get in a line behind them. You are then ready to start the game.

FOLLOW-UP

As soon as the new lines have been formed, you can check that the order is roughly correct by asking a few key questions. If there are two or more lines you can ask learners from the beginning, middle and end to have impromptu conversations to check how the lines compare.

Learners could prepare a short statement about their knowledge of computers using material of the activity and making comparisons with other members of the group. This could be written, or presented orally in front of the class.

VARIATIONS

GET IN LINE can be used with any language area that involves comparisons or measurement. For example:

★ *How far do you live from the centre of London?*
★ *How early do you get up on Sunday morning?*
★ *How healthy is your diet?*

Type: Whole-group activity	THE RUSSIAN TRAVELLING SALESMAN
Timing: At least 30 minutes	*by John Langran*

★ To practise future tenses, and in Russian to revise the use of the locative case. To practise the use of language associated with making arrangements to meet. **PURPOSE**

★ The game was devised for use with intermediate groups in Russian who needed practice with future tenses. It can be adapted for similar purposes with a different title for any language and the strategy can be reused with different scenarios. More advanced learners can be asked to develop the situations, adding as much detail as they can. **LANGUAGE ELEMENTS**

Prepare a blank calendar and make a copy of it for every member of the group. **PREPARATION**

ЯНВАРЬ

ФЕВРАЛЬ

МАРТ

АПРЕЛЬ

МАЙ

ИЮНЬ

ИЮЛЬ

АВГУСТ

СЕНТЯБРЬ

ОКТЯБРЬ

НОЯБРЬ

ДЕКАБРЬ

ПАРИЖ	ЛОНДОН	НЬЮ-ЙОРК

Calendar for the Russian travelling salesman with twelve months of the year and three towns.

PRE-TEACHING

For the Russian version, the game is intended to be used after the introduction of the two future tenses. Learners should practise:

★ Где вы будете в январе? (Where will you be in January?)
★ Где мы встретимся? (Where shall we meet?)
★ Как я вас узнаю? (How will I recognise you?)

In Russian, learners are also likely to need revision of the use of the locative case with places and with months of the year, and the stress on the endings of the months themselves. Other languages will have their own difficulties.

ACTIVITY

Tell the learners that they are (Russian) travelling salespeople, working overseas. To set the scene, ask them to decide what they are selling. Give suggestions if necessary. Talk about how miserable the life of a travelling salesman can be. Just one month of holiday with the family, the rest of the year spent in different cities, living in hotels, with no social contacts. Give out a calendar (illustrated above) and ask learners to decide which cities they are going to spend their time in. First they choose their month's holiday, then they plan the rest of their year. At this stage you may ask them to think of one or two things that they would really like to do or see in each city. All this information they write on their calendar.

Now explain that while their life is really a very boring and lonely one, today is an excellent opportunity to do something about this, because today is the annual meeting of (Russian) travelling salesmen. While they are together they have a chance to find out who they can meet up with during the rest of the year. Their task is to talk to other learners and try to find people who are going to be in the same city at the same time as themselves, then arrange when to meet and where, how to recognise each other, and one or two things they can do together. They can of course add anything else to the conversation, including talking about what they are selling.

LOGISTICS

Be careful with the number of towns you offer. Even with a large group, three is probably enough. With larger groups you should suggest that people try to meet no more than twice during the year; with smaller groups this may not be necessary. There is no need to let everyone fill his or her calendar. It is more effective to stop the game early.

Make sure learners don't try to read each other's calendar. They should be able to complete the task just by talking.

Ask who has a nearly full calendar. Then ask him or her to say what he or she is going to do with whom, when, etc. Then ask someone to say for which months/cities they have not been able to find a partner. At this stage someone is bound to offer to meet them and you are likely to have a spontaneous free conversation in front of the whole group.

There is clearly an opportunity for a written follow-up: learners to write a summary of their calendar. You may choose to do this if you want to be sure that learners have control of the correct future tense forms.

The principle of filling in a diary can be reused in a range of different imagined situations. For example, you are going to be living for a week in Moscow; arrange an outing with a different member of the group for each day of the week. This can be turned into a major simulation with town maps and information, and even an imaginary tourist information office.

I LOVE... *by John Langran*	**Type:** Game in a circle **Timing:** Approx 10 minutes

PURPOSE	★ Intensive repetition of a single structure.
LANGUAGE ELEMENTS	★ The game was devised to practise the present tense of the verb 'to love'. In Russian Я люблю (I love) is difficult and memorable for beginners. In French the game might be useful to practise the pronunciation of the R in *J'adore*. In Italian it can be used to drill *mi piace/mi piacciono*, and in Spanish the use of pronouns with *encantar*. Also to practise infinitives and, in inflected languages, to practise accusative endings.

PRE-TEACHING   Intensive practice of the point you want to stress, depending on the language. Practice of the intonation and use of the phrase 'me too'.

ACTIVITY   Ask your group to stand in a circle. If the group is larger than sixteen, perhaps two circles. Start by asking everybody to think about something they really like: chocolate, singing in the rain, playing golf, fishing, folk dancing, vodka - whatever, as long as they can say it. New words can be written on the board as they come up.

First, round the circle, everyone says one thing that they like. They make a chain, gradually building up, with each learner adding something they like (see MY GRANDMOTHER WENT TO MARKET, page 48).

Then ask the group if they can remember what other learners liked. Ask about each in turn. By this time learners will have committed a lot to memory.

Now ask for silence. Say that everyone has mentioned something they like, but you are sure that they like more than one thing. Ask them to catch the eye of others in the group whose likes they share; a nod or a wink to make contact in absolute silence. This creates a bond between people.

Now ask them to go and talk to the people they have nodded to. Ask them to use the phrase *me too* and to compare notes on what they like. Learners mill around in a group talking to each other.

If you also want to practise the third person of the verb, after a few minutes you can ask learners to turn to a neighbour and talk about the likes of other people in the room. If you had two circles you could ask learners to work in pairs, one from each circle, to compare the likes of both groups.

You need to keep a fairly strict discipline, particularly at the start of the game. You need to be sure that everyone understands any new nouns or verbs that are introduced. Be ready to write them on the board and stop the activity to rehearse their pronunciation.

Be careful not to put nervous learners under too much pressure when they are working in the full circle. Help people out if they can't remember everything. Correct mistakes gently.

The exercise leads naturally to an oral summary with the whole group, or a written homework.

The same sequence of activities can be used with other verbs. For example to hate, to live in, to like eating, to play (sports, instruments) and so on, and could be used with other tenses: future, past and conditional.

The principle of repetition in the circle is particularly useful with items that are proving difficult to pronounce. Suppose your group is having problems with the pronunciation of the French *Je téléphonerai* (I will telephone). In the circle you can ask learners to each say that they will telephone at a different time, and then ask everyone to remember the times. Then you could ask them to nod to a person who they think is going to telephone at a time close to theirs, and go and check.

Some teachers like to ask their learners to hold hands while they are in a circle, to establish contact and greater trust.

LE DOURDY *by John Langran*	**Type:** Picture differences **Timing:** At least 30 minutes
PURPOSE	★ This example is used at the beginning of a one-week residential course in Brittanny. The learners are going to be staying at the Centre shown in the cartoon. It is therefore an extremely relevant exercise for practising some of the vocabulary they will need during the week. It is also valuable for developing descriptive skills, revising comparisons, prepositions and the use of *de* after the negative, and for general revision.
LANGUAGE ELEMENTS	★ Descriptive language with close attention to details.

Picture differences are used regularly in language teaching and sometimes incorporated into coursebooks.

Most frequently, teachers are happy to limit their work with picture differences to straightforward pair work. The teacher prepares two versions of the same picture, but there are a number of differences. Give half the class one version, and half the other. Put them in pairs, opposite each other, and ask them to find the differences, but without looking at their partner's picture.

This example, which was developed for Brasshouse Centre courses in Loctudy, Brittany, shows how the original idea can be effectively extended with collaborative group work.

PREPARATION

Prepare copies of the two versions of the picture (see pages 37/38) on different coloured paper. You need enough copies to give one version to half the class and the other version to the others. Clipboards are useful for resting on. Have a flipchart or board ready. Ideally, you need a room with flexible seating arrangements.

PRE-TEACHING

If you are confident that some of the group know most of the necessary language, no pre-teaching is needed. In this particular case specialist words such as *biniou* (Breton bagpipe) and *coiffe* will need to be explained.

Divide the learners into an even number of roughly equal-sized groups. Two groups of eight or four groups of seven, for example. Ask each group to choose a secretary. Then hand out the pictures. All of the members of each group have the same colour paper. Explain that the groups will be working together as a team, and ask the secretaries to spend five minutes checking that all members of the group know the vocabulary of the pictures.

ACTIVITY

When this time is up, ask people to leave their groups and find a colleague with a different coloured picture. They should sit or stand opposite each other and talk to each other about the pictures, looking for differences in the traditional way and marking them on their sheets. Go round and check that things are running smoothly. Be on hand to help, and make sure learners are not looking at each other's pictures.

There are thirteen differences in these pictures. When some pairs have found about eight differences, ask everyone to stop and go back to their original groups. We now have a situation where different learners in the same group know of different differences - a perfect information gap. Ask the secretaries to collate this information and try to make a list of the thirteen differences.

When they are ready, or before, ask the secretaries to come to the front of the class. They now tell you the differences their group has listed, possibly gaining one point for a correct difference and another for correct language. You can decide whether the secretaries should do this with their notes or without. In either case, the groups can be allowed to call out with assistance if necessary. The teacher brings all of this together and works out a final score, endeavouring, if possible of course, to achieve a draw.

There is likely to be confusion over right and left. The right hand side of the castle is the left hand side of the picture as you look at it. Attempts to clarify this in advance are likely to lead to even more confusion, however! Two differences that are sometimes missed: one picture is signed and the other isn't, and the papers are different colours!

CAUTION

There is a clear opportunity for a written follow-up describing the pictures, or listing the differences.

FOLLOW-UP

THE PICNIC *by John Langran*	**Type:** Collaborative activity **Timing:** Approx 30 minutes
PURPOSE	★ To practise asking and answering questions in Russian of the type У вас есть... ? (Have you...?), or in French to practise *du, de la, des* with food vocabulary. The exercise is particularly useful revision, for example as part of a day or short intensive course.
LANGUAGE ELEMENTS	★ Food vocabulary and basic questions and answers in the present tense.

PREPARATION

Decide how you want to divide up your class into groups for the exercise. Have a list of picnic vocabulary ready in case the class forgets something. One way of organising the game would be to prepare cards for the different items and ask learners to pick them, but this detracts from the 'ownership' factor (see page 11).

PRE-TEACHING

Tell the group they are all going on a picnic. Ask them to give you a list of things they need to take. Write the list on the board. Check pronunciation and use of the necessary structures.

ACTIVITY

This example is for Russian, but can easily be adapted. Tell the students they are going on a picnic, leaving Yaroslavsky station in Moscow at 10 o'clock in the morning. Ask them to divide into groups of three or four learners who are going to travel together. It is the evening before. Get them to talk about what they want to do, to get into the mood.

Then ask them to 'go home', i.e. sit back in their normal places. Then tell them that unfortunately they forgot to agree what they were each going to take as a contribution to the picnic. They have a problem. They don't know what to take because they don't know what the others are taking. Ask them to write down what they are going to take. Perhaps two items of food or drink, and one item of equipment each. Get them to do this silently, without consulting each other.

Now it is the following morning, 10 o'clock, and they are meeting at the station. Ask them to tell each other what they have brought with them. Have they what they need for a good picnic? Get them to check. Ask one group who thinks they have what they need to tell you what it is. Then suggest that perhaps they can improve their own picnic by talking to the other groups and swapping anything they have brought too much of. The amount of time you give for this will depend on the group.

Then ask another group to tell you what it has managed to get together.

You need a room with flexible seating and, if possible, a separate area for small group work, though this is not essential. It is important to judge carefully how many items you ask people to take. This will depend on the number of items you suggest they choose from, and the size of the groups. It must not be too easy to get together a good picnic first time.   LOGISTICS

Be sure people don't start to discuss who will buy what during the introduction when they are talking about going on the picnic 'tomorrow'.   CAUTION

Clearly learners can prepare a list of what they took and who took what. More advanced groups using the activity as revision could prepare an account of the picnic in the past tense.   FOLLOW-UP

The same technique lends itself to specialist language courses for business people where you can focus on a particular task that needs to be completed. For example, building a car or a boat, setting up an office, even recruiting a team of specialists for a particular job.   VARIATIONS

THE NOBEL PRIZE *by Natasha Markina**	**Type:** Simulation **Timing:** At least 30 minutes
PURPOSE	★ This is a dramatic simulation for free expression and invention, not linked to any particular language structures, but with plenty of opportunity for learners to recycle situational language that they have recently learned or practised, for example during an intensive residential course. It is a full dramatic simulation, and as such it puts learners in a situation where they will have to react to unexpected circumstances using the language they have available to them. It can therefore be quite a threatening experience, and should only be used with groups that you know can cope with it. But for these groups it is an excellent way of preparing for what will actually happen when they have to use a foreign language in real life.
LANGUAGE ELEMENTS	★ Free use of language. Learners must be prepared to take risks.

PREPARATION

There is no specific preparation for the group. It is important that there should be an element of surprise. The teacher should think carefully about who should take which role, and should prepare a letter to the person who is being awarded the Nobel Prize, as well as ideas for suggestions to make to other protagonists.

ACTIVITY

The teacher announces that a letter has come for a member of the group. He or she has to read it and explain to the others what it is about. The letter states that he or she has been awarded the Nobel Prize, for a particular reason, and asks whether he or she can come to Norway to collect it next Saturday. Then the teacher asks what the prizewinner will have to do before the trip, e.g.:

★ *Check with wife/husband that it's ok to go.*
★ *Ask for time off from work.*
★ *Go to see elderly aunt in hospital.*
★ *Explain to son that he or she can't watch him play in football final.*
★ *Check plane/train/boat times.*
★ *Get a new suit made quickly.*

---

* Natasha Markina is Senior Teacher of Russian at the Moscow organisation 'INNOTEC'.

★ *Buy a ticket.*
★ *Change some money.*

You are likely to get some more suggestions from the group.

Then quickly assign roles to other members of the group, e.g.:

★ spouse   ★ son   ★ travel enquiry staff
★ employer   ★ tailor   ★ bank staff
★ elderly aunt

Nominate someone to meet the prizewinner on arrival in Norway, and someone to present him or her with the prize. Write a list of the people on the board. Try to find a role for everyone, perhaps with some learners working in pairs.

The prizewinner's task is to have a conversation with everyone on the list, explaining about the prize and making the necessary arrangements. Give everyone as much time as necessary to prepare what they are going to say. Offer help with vocabulary. Stop everyone to explain any new words that come up. Suggest to the more able learners that they might perhaps invent some difficulties. You may add some yourself. The prizewinner misses the boat, for example, and has to find alternative travel at the last moment.

Then ask everyone to listen to the conversations in sequence, starting with the spouse and ending with the presentation of the Nobel Prize.

FOLLOW-UP

Clearly, if you have the time you can repeat the exercise several times with the same roles or having changed around. As this is theatre, learners may want to rehearse and then give a final performance. Learners may appreciate you recording some of their conversations on tape for playback and analysis.

There is plenty of opportunity for oral or written follow-up. Ask learners to give a straightforward account of what happened, or give one yourself, with some details missed out or changed for learners to add or correct.

VARIATIONS

For further simulations along the same lines you need to find other exciting scenarios which lead to a natural sequence of events.

Old favourites and other activities

Chapter 4

Old favourites adapted for adult language classes

There are a large number of popular games that can easily be adapted for language teaching purposes. We have made the assumption that most readers already know the basics of these traditional children's games. If you haven't come across a particular traditional British game before, and the instructions aren't clear, it is probably best to ask a colleague to go through it with you. It is also an interesting language exercise to get your (advanced) learners to explain the rules to you.

Most games require little preparation on the part of the teacher. HAPPY FAMILIES means preparing about forty cards for every four people in the class, but the book *A thousand pictures for teachers to copy* by Andrew Wright (Collins) has lots of pictures arranged by 'family' which can be copied.

HAPPY FAMILIES

This game is good for revising vocabulary as well as for practising ways of asking for things. It is best played in small groups - four is an ideal number. Each group uses a pack of about 40 cards, comprising ten 'families' of four items, e.g. four drinks, four means of transport, four pieces of furniture, four fruits, etc. Be sure that you explain in advance which four items each family contains, or write the other three items on each card.

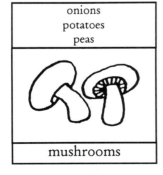

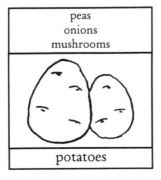

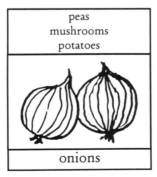

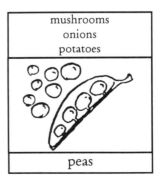

Pictures taken from *A thousand pictures for teachers to copy* by Andrew Wright (Collins)

Deal out the cards. Each player looks at his own hand. The aim is for players to collect entire families by requesting items in turn from each other, saying *Have you got... ? Please give me... . I'd like... .*

Explain the rules clearly, i.e. if it is your turn first, you ask another player if he holds the card you want. If he has it, he gives it to you, and you then have another turn. If he hasn't, he gives a suitable response, e.g. *No, I'm sorry, I haven't*, and it is then the next player's turn. You must hold at least one member of a family in your hand before you can start collecting that family. The winner is the person who collects the most whole families.

BINGO

This is a useful activity for checking or training listening comprehension of numbers or other language items, and is usually popular with adult groups.

Specify a series of numbers, say 60-100, bearing in mind how long you want the game to take. Ask each learner to write down four of the numbers. Then the teacher or an able member of the group calls out numbers from the series at random, and players cross out any of their numbers which are called. The first student to cross out all four numbers shouts something appropriate in the foreign language, perhaps *J'ai fini*. Check that the numbers which have been crossed off were actually called.

Time and date bingo are useful variations. Prepare a different card for each student with several clock faces or dates written as figures, as below. Make a separate list of about twenty times or dates to call, making sure that at least one of the students' cards will be a winner.

	2.3		31.1	
4.6		27.10		
	13.8			7.9

Any language structure or vocabulary items can be revised using the bingo format. For instance, students' cards could contain four past participles which they have to match to the infinitives you call out. For vocabulary practice, call out an item, say *cabbage* or *des fraises*, and students have to cross off the matching picture.

TWENTY QUESTIONS

This game, which is suitable for small group work or as an activity for the whole class, practises questions using the present tense. It is good for extending vocabulary.

One person thinks of a word; the rest of the group try to guess what it is by asking no more than twenty questions of the yes/no type. It is best to have a theme in the choice of word since then a limited range of useful language will be practised, e.g.:

Countries:	★ *Is this country big/far away?*
	★ *Do people there play rugby/speak English?*
Famous people:	★ *Are you a politician/American/a woman?*
Verbs:	★ *Do you do this in the morning/every day/in the garden?*

Either the teacher or a learner can choose the mystery word. If the group is at a loss for a suitable question or is going off on the wrong track you can chip in with a leading question to guide the students in the right direction.

WHAT'S MY LINE?

As TWENTY QUESTIONS, but here the mystery word is always a profession. Questions could include:

★ *Do you work inside or outside?*
★ *Do you wear a uniform?*
★ *Do you work nights?*
★ *Do you travel a lot?*

KIM'S GAME

This memory game is very useful for practising prepositions and colours, e.g.:

★ *The pen was next to the book.*
★ *The key was on top of the packet of cigarettes.*
★ *There were two red pencils but one green pencil.*

Work with the whole class or with groups. Arrange a number of objects on a tray and give learners a minute to study and memorise them. Then take the tray away or cover it. Learners have to remember what was on the tray.

Instead of a tray, you can use an overhead projector. Place a number of items with easily recognisable silhouettes onto the projector. Then switch off for a few seconds while you make a few changes. When you switch back on again learners say what has changed, perhaps using the passive:

★ *The matchstick has been broken.*
★ *The key has been moved.*
★ *Half the biscuit has been eaten.*

or the present perfect tense:

★ *You've put the coin in the purse.*
★ *You've moved the ring.*

MY GRANDMOTHER WENT TO MARKET...

This is an excellent short exercise at the drilling stage in the presentation of new material, or when teaching an item that needs intensive pronunciation practice. The activity is also very useful for reinforcing vocabulary and structures.

Stand or sit in a circle, or two or three small circles if the material is more difficult. Each student adds an item while remembering what has gone before. The traditional game goes as follows:

Learner 1:   *My grandmother went to market and bought some lemons.*
Learner 2:   *My grandmother went to market and bought some lemons and some apples.*
Learner 3:   *My grandmother went to market and bought some lemons, some apples and a melon.*
Learner 4:   *My grandmother went to market and bought some lemons, some apples, a melon and some grapes.*
and so on.

In order to practise a particular vocabulary area the context can be changed:

★ *My grandmother went to a furniture store and bought a chair (table, sofa, bed etc).*

★ *I went to a party and met a doctor (journalist, plumber, bank manager etc).*
★ *My grandmother went on holiday and packed a bikini (a pair of sunglasses, some soap, a camera etc).*

If you prefer, you can direct the vocabulary to be used by holding up the item itself or a picture.

Verbs can also be practised in a particular tense:

Learner 1:	*Yesterday I went to London and saw Big Ben.*
Learner 2:	*Yesterday I went to London, saw Big Ben and travelled on the tube.*
Learner 3:	*Yesterday I went to London, saw Big Ben, travelled on the tube and went to Harrods.*
Learner 4:	*Yesterday I went to London, saw Big Ben, travelled on the tube, went to Harrods and bought a new dress.*

and so on.

Other short activities

The following suggestions for shorter activities can be used to practise particular language points as needed, and are also suitable for those times when you realise that you have run out of material for a particular lesson and need an idea quickly.

No advance preparation is required and no complicated instructions or rearrangement of furniture are needed.

FIND SOMEONE/THE PERSON WHO...

In a lesson on time or the past tense, ask the learners to find someone who got up at the same time as they did or find the person who got up the earliest this morning. The learners must then move round the class asking everyone else *What time did you get up?*

The technique can be adapted to suit any language item, e.g:

Find someone who...

★ bought the same newspaper as you today;
★ has a birthday in the same month as you;
★ had an interesting holiday this year;
★ is doing something exciting next week;
★ lives near you;
★ shares your favourite hobby.

Find the person who...

★ is going to the most interesting place on holiday;
★ lives the furthest away;
★ is going on holiday the soonest;
★ had the most exciting weekend.

If you know any interesting snippets of information about individual learners, you can include them in your request to the class.

Find the person who...

★ plays the trumpet;
★ works for the Bank of England;
★ went to Hong Kong last summer.

Specify whether you want the students to ask a yes/no question, e.g. *Do you play the trumpet?* or an open question, e.g. *Where do you work? Where did you go on holiday last summer?*

Learners write a short sentence about themselves on a piece of paper. The sentence should relate to the language to be practised - so, if the theme is the past tense, ask learners to write a sentence about what they did today. If a German class has been learning the use of *seit* or a French class the use of *depuis*, they will write a sentence using this word.

Move around the class as everyone is writing and correct any mistakes.

I got up at 7.30am.

Ich bin seit 8 Jahren verheiratet.

J'habite Liverpool depuis 15 ans.

I met my sister for lunch.

Collect all the pieces of paper, jumble them up and redistribute them so that each learner is looking at someone else's sentence. The aim is for each learner to find the person who wrote 'his/her' sentence by turning it into a yes/no type question and questioning the rest of the class:

★ *Did you get up at half past seven this morning?*
★ *Did you meet your sister for lunch today?*
★ *Sind Sie seit 8 Jahren verheiratet?*
★ *Vous habitez Liverpool depuis quinze ans?*

Clearly you need to take care with this exercise that the sentences have been written correctly, both because you don't want people to copy each other's mistakes, and because you don't want to embarrass anyone who might make a public howler.

ORDERING GAME

which makes us want to speak, and this can be exploited by the language teacher. Choose a process that has a logical sequence:

★ Getting up in the morning.
★ Making a cup of tea.
★ Arranging to go away on holiday.

Write out the things that need to be done, but in a jumbled order. For the cup of tea:

❑ Pour the milk into the cup.
❑ Pour the tea into the cup.
❑ Boil the kettle.
❑ Fill the kettle with water.
❑ Pour the boiling water into the pot.
❑ Warm the pot.
❑ Put the tea in the pot.
❑ Let the tea stand.

First ask the learners, working in pairs, to put things in the right order by putting a number against each sentence. Then perhaps take the papers away and ask them to repeat the task from memory.

This technique can be used with any narrative text with a logical order and is particularly useful with more advanced groups for handling narrative newspaper articles. Cut the article up into small sections and ask pairs to put it together again.

Try the example below. It is most effective working as a pair or a small group. You then have to agree about the order, which means you are forced to talk about it. This example is particularly effective in English classes after listening to the Gerard Hoffnung recording.

❏ I started to come down at high speed.
❏ It hit me on the shoulder, causing a nasty bruise.
❏ Then I went back down and cast off the line.
❏ Half way up I met the barrel coming down.
❏ I rigged up a beam, a pulley, a rope and a barrel, to carry them down.
❏ It started to come down, jerking me suddenly off my feet.
❏ I respectfully request sick leave.
❏ I then went back to the top of the building and filled the barrel with bricks.
❏ When I reached the top I banged my head on the beam and caught my fingers in the pulley.
❏ I hoisted the barrel up to the top and fastened the line at the bottom.
❏ When the barrel reached the ground, it burst, allowing the bricks to spill out.
❏ I was now heavier than the barrel.
❏ When the building was finished there were some bricks left over at the top.
❏ Half way down I met the barrel coming up, receiving a nasty blow on the shin.
❏ I continued down and landed on the bricks, breaking my left ankle.
❏ At this point I must have lost my presence of mind, for I let go of the rope.
❏ I decided to hang on.
❏ The barrel fell on my head, knocking me unconscious.
❏ Unfortunately the barrel was heavier than I was.

Of course the difficulty for this type of activity is finding suitable material for your language at the right level. However, it does exist and you should try to build your own collection. Narrative poetry can be effectively used in this way, as the rhyme and rhythm assist the memory process. In French the poems of Jacques Prévert are a good example, especially *Café du matin*.

Adapted from *The Bricklayer* story as told by Gerard Hoffnung in *Hoffnung, a last encore*, BBC Radio Collection

Board games

Commercially produced board games using dice or cards can be useful for advanced conversation work with advanced learners who have the necessary time. MONOPOLY and CLUEDO type games are particularly useful and several word games, such as SCRABBLE, are available in different languages.

Adapting party games

Do not limit yourself to looking at language textbooks for ideas. Many traditional party games, particularly those which are designed to be ice-breakers played as guests arrive, are ideal for talking to one another in any language.

In one example, suitable for intermediate groups, a piece of paper with the name of a famous person is pinned to the back of each guest; he/she cannot see it but everyone else can. The aim is to guess who you are by asking the other guests *Am I a man? Am I a sportsman?* etc.

Similarly, in FIND YOUR PARTNER, each guest is told he is one half of a famous couple and has to find his partner by asking *Are you Russian? Are you a character in a book? Are you alive now?* and so on. Napoleon has to find Josephine and Laurel has to find Hardy. Be careful that you do not embarrass members of the group by over-estimating their general knowledge! And stop them just asking *Are you Josephine?*

Any adults' or children's party games book will contain a wealth of thought-provoking ideas.

Adapting radio and television games

TWENTY QUESTIONS (page 46) started out as a radio game, and WHAT'S MY LINE? was a popular television programme in the sixties. Current quiz shows and panel games, particularly those broadcast on radio where the spoken word is all important, can frequently be adapted for the language learning classroom. JUST A MINUTE, in which people have to talk for a minute on a chosen topic without hesitation or repetition, is an excellent device for advanced conversation classes, as is CALL MY BLUFF, in which learners have to think up a plausible definition for an unknown word in the target language. Many other panel games are likely to give you new ideas for communicative activities.

Using a soft toy

This is a way of breaking down inhibitions and adding variety to a language drill, while getting learners to answer spontaneously and quickly.

Make sure that whatever language you are drilling has been thoroughly learnt. Then stand in circles, perhaps no more than six in each, with a soft toy or a soft ball (one that won't bounce if dropped) in each circle. Learners throw the toy to each other at random. The thrower asks a question using the structure you have been teaching, and the catcher has to answer.

Structures can be as simple as *What's your name?* or as complicated as you wish, although the activity is best appreciated by beginners' groups.

An alternative is to choose a vocabulary topic, e.g. the bathroom. Each player who catches the toy has to give a word relating to the topic: bath, towel, shower, sponge, etc. If a learner cannot add a word he or she drops out until one winner is left.

Overcoming resistance to language games

Chapter 5

You may meet resistance to language games from learners, from other teachers and from organisations where you teach. The following should provide you with some ideas of how to overcome this resistance.

I don't like pair work with people who keep making mistakes

This is a difficult argument to counter. It needs to be said that you should avoid asking groups to use material which they have not mastered for free role play activities. Many of the activities which encourage co-operation also encourage peer support and correction.

When using pair work, try to arrange for learners to work with different partners as much as possible. It is difficult to insist on this with nervous learners, but as confidence develops it should be normal procedure.

I simply don't like all that standing up and prancing around

It is difficult to get groups used to working actively and moving around the classroom, especially on the first few occasions. One way of encouraging this is to pin workcards that people need for a particular assignment around the wall. Then students have to get up and look at them. Learners are likely to feel self-conscious the first time they are asked to stand around in a circle. Try to keep the atmosphere as relaxed as possible. Also remember that there could well be people in the group who can't move around too much because of physical problems which may or may not be immediately apparent.

Not all learners will share your enthusiasm for language games. One or two may think they are silly or a waste of time, believing that old-fashioned teaching methods are best. If you can explain why you are playing a particular game and what linguistic item or skill you want to practise, people may see your point. However, you can't force people to join in if they don't want to. Learners who want to be in the class but not

From learners

participate in the language games, can watch, keep score, check mistakes, act as umpire, or get on with some other activity if they want to.

If you are worried about a possible negative reaction from a new group, it may be a good idea not to use the word 'game' when you introduce the activity. For example, when introducing THE PICNIC you can say something like 'Now we are going to apply the language we've just been practising in a situation you might meet when you go abroad. Imagine you are going on a picnic....'.

From teachers

There isn't enough time for this sort of work

This is fair comment. Adult education groups in the UK often have only 1½ hours per week and only 25 or 30 weeks a year.

However, language games do provide a way of using the available time very effectively, with more learners using the language for communicative purposes more of the time. Many of the games in this book take only five or ten minutes to play. And many examination syllabuses contain role plays which can be prepared effectively with games techniques.

There is too much preparation

A number of the activities described in this book do require a lot of detailed preparation. However, once this has been done the material can easily be reused with different groups. Other activities demand only a minimum or even no written preparation at all, for example I LOVE... (page 34).

Keep a separate file for each new language game you prepare, and consider the advantages of pooling such resources with other teachers.

I simply haven't got a suitable room to work in. I can't move the furniture around because it's used by someone else the next morning

This is of course a frequent difficulty, not only in classes for adults. In general, though, educational administrators in all sectors are becoming more aware of the needs of up-to-date teaching methods, and a well-reasoned request for the right sort of accommodation long enough in advance is likely to get a sympathetic hearing.

Most adult groups will gladly help to move furniture around and put it back afterwards. This fosters group spirit and can be done in the language you are teaching.

All of the above points may be used by teaching organisations where there is resistance to new ideas. By now we think that most language teaching centres have decided to opt for communicative approaches. Most centres will have a policy on the issue. You need to get the balance right and use the mechanisms that exist in the organisation that employs you to discuss the approaches you use with your groups and to obtain support where necessary.

From organisations

Over to you

Chapter 6

We hope that having read this book you will try out some of the games and activities with your classes. But we hope that you will not stop there. All the games and activities can be adapted to be used with different languages and in different contexts. We have made some suggestions for varying and extending the games. We hope that we have set you thinking of more ways in which the activities can be adapted to suit your learners.

You may find it useful to ask yourself the following questions:

- How often do you use language games?
- For what purposes?
- Do you want to use them more or do you think you should use them less?
- How do you justify their use?
- Are there any routine activities you currently use that you could replace with a language game?
- Do the coursebooks you currently use suggest language games for each chapter? If no, can you devise suitable games? If yes, can you think of more?
- As a learner of languages do you think you would appreciate an approach that emphasises the use of language games?

If you are involved in a local NETWORD group, these questions could form the basis of a training session on language games. One effective way to start such a session would be to use GET IN LINE (page 29) with the question 'How often do you use language games?'.

Games and progression

The use of language games with individual classes can be planned to give you and your learners an opportunity to assess the progress being made.

Many games can be used at different levels, and it can be very effective to use a particular game twice with the same group, perhaps with a gap of several weeks or months between the sessions. This gives learners an opportunity to become aware of the progress they have made in terms of increased fluency and facility in the language and a larger active vocabulary.

Records that you keep of such reactions are useful for documenting the progress your learners are making.

| | Developing your repertoire |

As you become more experienced at using language games you will begin to see opportunities for developing simple scenarios in order to make a particular activity more motivating.

For example, look at the activity CONTRABAND on page 13. Can you think of a way to adapt this, introducing more dramatic tension and involvement by giving travellers an opportunity to lie to the customs officers, but still keeping the whole activity under control? (Turn to page 60 for a suggested answer.)

Feedback from learners

You will probably find it useful and revealing to ask your learners from time to time how they found a particular activity:

- Did they enjoy it?
- Did they find it appropriate?
- Did they understand the instructions fully?
- Did they find the language element too easy/too difficult?
- Did they understand the other learners properly?
- Did they find the game a challenge?
- Did they have the sort of conversations that they would expect to have in real life?
- Would they want to do it again?

Pool your resources

New ideas for the classroom can take up large amounts of time and energy in preparation. However, as you become more used to using language games you will find you are able to think up scenarios and judge the logistics more quickly and effectively. It will also save time if you consider pooling your resources locally, and you could consider using your local NETWORD group or main language centre as a base for a collection of materials, role-cards, and ideas for language games. This may involve as little extra work as making a photocopy of material as you devise it and filing it.

In the same way a group of teachers can share a collection of some of the excellent books available on language games (see Further reading, page 60). Many of these include photocopiable role playing material. Do not limit yourself to books aimed at teachers only of your particular language. Games in other languages can easily be adapted or translated.

One possible extension of CONTRABAND	To adapt CONTRABAND to a more exciting activity where 'travellers' are allowed to lie about what they are carrying through customs, and the 'customs officers' have to try to find them out, you need a fairly tight control on what is actually permitted. One way of doing this would be to allow 'travellers' to lie about three items only, and to tell the 'customs officer' that they can use the questions *Etes-vous sûr?* just three times with each 'traveller'. After that, the 'travellers' have to tell the truth.

Further reading

Dahl P, K Smith and H Myers, *Actif 1* (Nelson, 1989)

Friedrich T and E von Jan, *Games cards - communicative activities for English language classes* (Max Hueber Verlag, 1993)

Granger C, *Play games with English* (Heinemann International)

Hadfield J, *Harrap's communication games: elementary/intermediate/advanced* (Nelson)

Lee W R, *Language teaching games and contests* (OUP, 1979)

Lewis M, *Partners* (Language Teaching Publications)

McGinnis S et al, *Let's play games in Japanese* (NTC, 1992; distributed by European Schoolbooks)

Mini-flashcards language games (1991; revised 1993) - various packs in French, German, Spanish, Italian and Russian. Written for children but useful for adult groups.

Rinvolucri M, *Grammar games* (CUP, 1984)

Ur P, *Discussions that work* (CUP, 1981)

Ur P, *Grammar practice activities: a practical guide for teachers* (CUP, 1988)

Ur P and A Wright, *Five-minute activities: a resource book of short activities* (CUP, 1992)

Watcyn-Jones P, *Pair work: activities for effective communication* (Penguin, 1981)

Wright A, *A thousand pictures for teachers to copy* (Collins, 1984)